Monkey Mind

Story by Albert Nguyen
Illustrated by Quin Nguyen

A journey of a thousand miles begins with a single step.

- Lao Tzu -

Dedicated to all the children around the world.

Once upon a long ago, there lived a boy named Bai. But people called him "Monkey Mind," and here's the reason why.

Young Bai was such an antsy kid. A restless soul was he.
Just like the monkeys overhead that leaped from tree to tree.

His brain was a kaleidoscope of worry, doubt, and fears.
A swirling, twirling, tangled mess of thoughts and wild
ideas.

He also got quite moody, full of anger, tears, and stress.
Confusion would surround him, and his friends were not
impressed.

He found it hard to fall asleep or even settle down. Instead,
he'd find a million things that made him fret and frown.

5

In school, he couldn't concentrate and often fell behind.
His teacher lost patience, saying, "Come on, Monkey Mind."

His mom and dad would do their best to help him when they could. But though they tried to calm him down, it never did much good.

The elders of the village didn't seem to have a clue. "This boy
has got a monkey mind. Oh, what are we to do?

Perhaps he needs a potion or a little yellow pill? Or maybe he's pretending, and he isn't really ill?"

But Bai was not pretending, and inside his monkey mind, he decided to go wandering to see what he could find.

He journeyed over land and sea for many days and nights,
in search of information that could help him with his plight.

Until at last, he came upon an ancient dragon land, where high
upon a mountain top there lived a wise old man.

"I've come in search of knowledge, sir," the little boy explained.
"I need to tame my monkey mind. It's causing me such pain."

The wise old man spoke kindly, staring deep into his soul.
"The secret to a cure," he said, "is taking back control."

When monkey chatter clouds your mind, Don't listen to that voice. The way you feel is up to you. You have a choice.

You can't control the future, and the past is dead and gone.
So focus on the present, and you really can't go wrong."

"But how?" said Bai, frustrated. "This is tearing me apart.
I really want to change my ways but I don't know where to
start."

"Begin your day," the old man said, "by writing down your thoughts. It frees your cluttered mind from trash of many different sorts.

And practice mindfulness, my friend. Just focus on one thing. Breathe slowly, deeply in and out, and calmness it will bring.

Then, stop and spare a thought or two, for all the things you've got. A moment spent in gratitude will help you quite a lot."

"But what if I just can't?" said Bai, a tear upon his face.
"Then close your eyes," the old man said, "and find your happy place."

When Bai got home, he soon found out the old man's words were true. By doing all that he'd been told, his life began anew.

20

He was nowhere near as anxious. He was in control and calm.
Instead of being angry he was full of love and charm.

He grew to be a leader; clear of thought, relaxed, and kind. And all because he learned the way to tame his monkey mind.

Review Questions

P.01 - What did they call Bai?
P.02 - What was Bai like?
P.03 - What was Bai's brain like?
P.04 - What other feelings did Bai have?
P.05 - Why does Bai find it hard to fall asleep?
P.06 - Why does Bai's teacher lose patience?
P.07 - What does Bai's parents try to do? Did it work?
P.08 - What does the elders of the village say about Bai?
P.09 - Why do you think the elders think Bai needed a potion or a yellow pill?
P.10 - What did Bai decide to do?
P.11 - What was Bai searching for?
P.12 - How did Bai find the old wise man?
P.13 - What did Bai asked from the old wise man?
P.14 - What was the cure according to the old wise man?
P.15 - What can Bai do when his mind is clouded?
P.16 - What did the old wise man say about the past and future?
P.17 - How can Bai start his day?
P.18 - How can Bai practice mindfulness? What else can he do?
P.19 - What was the last thing Bai can do if he found it hard?
P.20 - What did Bai find out when he came back home?
P.21 - How did Bai change?
P.22 - What happened when Bai got older?

Message to Parents

Learning to manage our emotions begins when we are young and continues throughout our lives. By teaching your kids healthy coping strategies early on and practicing them regularly, you can build their resilience and set them up for success. Teaching your child healthy coping strategies can help them manage their stress and navigate life's ups and downs with a bit more ease and grace.

Lessons

In the story, Bai uses different strategies, known as coping skills, to manage his "monkey mind." Learning simple coping skills and practicing them daily is key. Like Bai, practicing small daily actions can lead to big positive changes.

Now it's your turn to help your child develop healthy strategies and skills!

Practice Guidelines

• **Practice healthy coping skills yourself.** Kids learn best from what they see, not just from what they're told. Good or bad, kids learn how to cope with challenges by watching the adults around them. If they see you coping in healthy ways, they're more likely to do the same.

• **Teach new coping strategies when everyone is calm.** It's difficult for a child to learn something new when they're upset, so avoid introducing a new coping skill in the middle of a meltdown or stressful situation.

• **Try lots of different coping skills.** Every coping strategy isn't going to work for every person, and what works today might not work tomorrow. That's why it's important for you and your kids to practice a variety of strategies to find what works best at any given time.

• **Build coping skills into your daily routine.** If practicing coping skills becomes a habit or part of your kids' everyday lives, they're more likely to use them without even realizing it.

• **Make practicing coping skills fun.** Make the most out of what kids already enjoy doing. Get creative by finding fun ways for your child to learn and practice coping skills through songs, games, play and more.

COPING SKILLS

Coping skills create a space between an emotion and an action to help your child calm down and respond in a healthy way.

Here are some simple coping skills to try:

1. Deep Breathing

a. Deep breathing is the most accessible relaxation technique because it is available to anyone at any time. It is the one thing that everyone is an expert in. When a person slows down and takes deeper breaths, it provides immediate and long-term benefits to alleviate stress and anxiety.

b. To breathe deeply, inhale slowly through your nose for 4 seconds. Then, pause and hold the air in your lungs for 4 seconds. After that, exhale slowly through your nose or mouth for 4 seconds. Repeat this cycle at least six times.

c. Breath control can be hard to teach young kids, so a creative way to teach deep breathing is by blowing bubbles! This fun and simple breathing exercise reinforces deep breathing and breath control. Deep and intentional breathing can promote calmness, reduce stress, and teach kids to regain control of their bodies when things feel out of control.

2. 5-4-3-2-1 Grounding Exercise

a. Grounding techniques are mental exercises that help redirect thoughts away from distressing feelings.

b. The 5-4-3-2-1 exercise is a simple and effective technique that kids of all ages can do. Try this by activating your senses and counting backward from 5 to identify:
    5 things you can hear
    4 things you can see
    3 things you can touch
    2 things you can smell
    1 thing you can taste

3. **Gratitude**

Studies have found that gratitude is linked to happiness in children as young as five, meaning that grateful children grow up to be happier people with a better quality of life.

- One of the easiest ways to practice gratitude is to encourage your child to say 'thank you' on a regular basis. You can also encourage them to write thank you cards.

  - For example, offer gentle reminders such as, "It was very nice of your friend to share her food with you. What should you say to her?"
  - "What do you say to Grandpa for giving you his favorite book?"

- When your child shows gratitude WITHOUT a prompt from you, make sure to praise them. This will encourage them to do so more often.

4. **Go Beyond Good Manners**

Ask your kids questions to nurture a deeper sense of gratitude:

1. What do you have in your life to be thankful for?

2. What do you think went well today? Did anything or anyone do something today that was special to you?

3. How does it make you feel when someone gives you a gift?

4. Is there a way to show how you feel?

The purpose of asking gentle questions is to explore and deepen their feelings of gratitude.

Model gratitude whenever you have the chance. Grateful parents who practice gratitude themselves tend to raise grateful kids. So, say 'thank you,' point out things you are thankful for, and express gratitude to your child when they are kind or helpful.

5. Name That Emotion

One of the first steps to managing difficult emotions is connecting words to feelings and being aware when they show up inside of us. Help your child practice using 'I feel' statements to identify how they are feeling. For example, 'I feel' angry, sad, or afraid.

6. The STOP Technique

This common technique teaches kids to take small breaks to check in with themselves and reset. The premise behind the STOP skill is to 'think before you act.' It involves four steps:

i.   Stop
ii. Take a deep breath
iii. Observe
iv. Proceed mindfully

Final Message

It's important to let your child know that anxiety can't hurt them.

Feelings of anxiety are safe, normal, and should be encouraged. By creating space for anxiety, we become more aware of the signals of distress. This helps us learn how to cope and decide what action to take.

In the end, the best way to introduce healthy coping skills to your child is to get involved, engage with them creatively, and make it a priority for the family to practice together.

If you're concerned about your child's stress levels and general emotional state, you may wish to connect with a child therapist or psychologist who can help you develop a treatment plan to improve your child's well-being.

Additional resources are available at www.optimindcounseling.com/resources.

About the Author

Albert Nguyen, LCSW, PPSC

With more than two decades of practicing as a licensed psychotherapist and martial artist, Albert Nguyen is passionate about raising awareness of children's mental health issues. As someone who struggled with anxiety during his childhood, Albert hopes to share his knowledge and wisdom to make a difference in the lives of children, parents, and guardians. He ultimately believes that simplicity is the best policy in teaching others important life skills.

Albert aims to enchant and inspire readers to feel confident, strong, and believe in themselves. This book is a passion project that marks his first venture into writing a children's book. With a touch of culturally relevant concepts and illustrations, Albert advocates for diversity and representation in literature. He hopes this book encourages parents and guardians to get involved and engage with their children in creative ways to break the stigma of common mental health problems. Words can't explain how deeply important the message of this story is to him.

To learn more about Albert and his mission, visit his website at www.optimindcounseling.com.

About the Illustrator

Quin Nguyen

As a young child growing up in a poverty-stricken household deep in the ghetto of old Sacramento, Quin didn't have much in the way of extravagant toys. His imagination was mostly all he had, as he plays at an old run-down playground close to his home or ride his beat-up red bike up and down the road, exploring unknown parts of the neighborhood where he would imagine himself as an explorer or an adventurer.

With his creative mind always on the loose, he began to learn about art during his down time when he wasn't outside. He would become the hero of his own story in these pencil sketches. It slowly became an outlet for him to express himself through the most difficult times during his childhood, where he learned to grow up quickly to take care of his younger siblings when his parents weren't around.

Today, art still remains a big part of his life where he likes to capture the essence of life through his own experiences or from those around him. He specializes in creating environment art with the occasional animal or character drawing. His art style can be described as traditional meets digital art, where he combines the best of both worlds in one fluid and unique illustration.

You can learn more about Quin and his artwork by visiting:
https://enterthesketch.artstation.com/
https://instagram.com/enterthesketch

Printed in Great Britain
by Amazon

58663658R00021